Seven Steps to Spiritual Stability

Seven Steps to Spiritual Stability

by
John MacArthur, Jr.

"GRACE TO YOU"
P.O. Box 4000
Panorama City, CA 91412

©1991 by
JOHN F. MACARTHUR, JR.

ISBN: 0-8024-5331-7

1 2 3 4 5 Printing/LC/Year 95 94 93 92 91

Printed in the United States of America

Contents

These Bible studies are taken from messages delivered by Pastor-Teacher John MacArthur, Jr., at Grace Community Church in Sun Valley, California. These messages have been combined into a six-tape album titled *Seven Steps to Spiritual Stability*. You may purchase this series either in an attractive vinyl cassette album or as individual cassettes. To purchase these tapes, request the album *Seven Steps to Spiritual Stability*, or ask for the tapes by their individual GC numbers. Please consult the current price list; then send your order, making your check payable to:

"GRACE TO YOU"
P.O. Box 4000
Panorama City, CA 91412

Or call the following toll-free number:
1-800-55-GRACE

1
Spiritual Stability—Introduction

Outline

A. The Presence of Instability
1. In today's church
2. In the Philippian church
B. The Concern About Instability
1. In the New Testament
   a) Shown by Christ
   b) Shown by Peter
   c) Shown by Paul
   d) Shown by James
2. In the Old Testament
C. The Biblical Command Regarding Stability
1. The necessity for the command
   a) Because of persecution
   b) Because of dissension
   c) Because of false teachers
2. The seriousness of the command
3. The basis of the command
   a) The believer's pursuit of Christlikeness
   b) Paul's care for the church
      (1) They were his love
      (2) They were his joy
      (3) They were his reward
4. The application of the command
   a) In Barnabas's ministry
   b) In Peter's ministry
   c) In Paul's ministry
   d) In Epaphras's ministry
5. The explanation of the command

A. The Presence of Instability

1. In today's church

I received a letter from a church leader who said, "My heart is broken because some friends have defaulted from the ministry." His letter is but one illustration of the widespread instability in today's church.

It's no surprise the church is under attack because Christ said it would be that way: "In this world you will have trouble" (John 16:33, NIV*). That trouble sometimes includes imprisonment and physical persecution for following Christ (Matt. 10:16-22).

Because the world, the flesh, and the devil are behind such hostility, Christ instructed us to "keep watching and praying, that [we] may not enter into temptation" (Matt. 26:41). Peter warned, "Be of sober spirit, be on the alert. Your adversary, the devil, prowls about like a roaring lion, seeking someone to devour" (1 Pet. 5:8). To be prepared, Paul said, "Let us be sober, having put on the breastplate of faith and love, and as a helmet, the hope of salvation" (1 Thess. 5:8).

Now it can be difficult to maintain your Christian testimony when persecution is subtle rather than open. I remember asking a Russian pastor, "What is it like to pastor a church in your country? Is it difficult?" The pastor responded, "No, it's easy because I know where everyone stands. But how can someone pastor a church in America, where compromise is so common and subtle?" Many so-called Christians want the world's acceptance and are therefore unwilling to take a stand for Christ.

The world is clever in its allurements, the flesh is vulnerable to temptation, and the devil is aggressive

---

* *New International Version.*

in his attack. So it's a battle to remain spiritually stable.

2. In the Philippian church

Paul and the Philippian believers shared a special love for each other (Phil. 1:8, 26; 4:15). Nevertheless, even that church experienced some instability.

Some of the believers were acting selfishly. Instead of thinking only of themselves, they needed to be like Christ (2:1-8). The church also experienced a lack of unity, illustrated by an intense disagreement between two women (4:2). It must have been serious since Paul identified them by name and asked for other believers to help correct the problem. Besides that, some in the church apparently struggled with depression, harshness of spirit, anxiety, failure to take prayer seriously, thanklessness, and wrong thought patterns (4:4-8).

B. The Concern About Instability

1. In the New Testament

   a) Shown by Christ

   Being a disciple of Christ would cost Peter his life (John 21:18). Nevertheless Christ said to him, "Follow Me!" (v. 19), encouraging him to be strong and steadfast in the face of persecution. To prevent any of His disciples from being shaken by the unexpected, Christ told them all to anticipate trials (Matt. 10:16-22).

   b) Shown by Peter

   Peter warned believers about false teachers, who were "enticing unstable souls" (2 Pet. 2:14). He repeatedly called them to heed sound doctrine so they would "never stumble" (1:10). He also instructed them to be on guard because "the untaught and unstable distort" the Scriptures (3:16-17).

c) Shown by Paul

Knowing false teachers would enter the churches, Paul strengthened the Ephesian believers by teaching them the Scriptures for three years (Acts 20:29-31).

d) Shown by James

James described the spiritually unstable as "double-minded" (1:8) because they vacillate between doubt and faith. Unsure of what they believe or what is right, they find it difficult to make decisions. To remove that kind of unsteadiness, James wanted the believers to have a true understanding of God's character (1:13-17).

2. In the Old Testament

The life of Reuben illustrates why we should be concerned about instability. As the oldest son in the patriarch Jacob's family, Reuben was to receive highly valued privileges such as a larger inheritance and a special paternal blessing. But Reuben's immorality (Gen. 35:22) showed him to be as "uncontrolled as water" (49:4). Therefore he forfeited his special privileges and ruined a promising future.

No Christian wants to be unstable and defeated by trials or temptation. So how can we stand firm?

C. The Biblical Command Regarding Stability

Paul begins Philippians 4 by saying, "Therefore, my beloved brethren whom I long to see, my joy and crown, so stand firm in the Lord, my beloved." That command to stand firm is the dominant theme of verses 1-9.

1. The necessity for the command

   a) Because of persecution

   Paul told the believers, "To you it has been granted for Christ's sake, not only to believe in Him, but also to suffer for His sake" (Phil. 1:29).

   b) Because of dissension

   To help counter any potential problem with dissension, Paul made these appeals:

   (1) Philippians 2:2—"Make my joy complete by being of the same mind, maintaining the same love, united in spirit, intent on one purpose."

   (2) Philippians 1:27—"Conduct yourselves in a manner worthy of the gospel of Christ; so that whether I come and see you or remain absent, I may hear of you that you are standing firm in one spirit, with one mind striving together for the faith of the gospel."

   (3) Philippians 2:14—"Do all things without grumbling or disputing."

   c) Because of false teachers

   (1) Philippians 3:2—"Beware of the dogs, beware of the evil workers, beware of the false circumcision." Judaizers added works to faith as a requirement for salvation—an unbiblical teaching.

   (2) Philippians 3:18-19—"They are enemies of the cross of Christ, whose end is destruction, whose god is their appetite, and whose glory is in their shame, who set their minds on earthly things." Others taught that good works weren't the necessary evidence of gen-

uine faith—another wrong teaching (cf. James 2:17).

2. The seriousness of the command

The Greek term translated "stand firm" in Philippians 4:1 is a military word that pictures a soldier standing his ground in the midst of battle. Paul uses the same metaphor in Ephesians 6:11: "Put on the full armor of God, that you may be able to stand firm against the schemes of the devil." Standing firm spiritually means not compromising your Christian testimony by allowing yourself to be overwhelmed by trials or temptation.

It saddens me that many believers don't take God and His commands seriously enough. Instead of wanting to know God, many prefer to be entertained. That kind of apathy regards His commands as mere suggestions. But our sovereign Lord commands us to stand firm. Inherent in that command is the capacity to obey.

3. The basis of the command

   a) The believer's pursuit of Christlikeness

   Philippians 4:1 says, "Therefore . . . stand firm." That refers back to chapter 3, which says to diligently pursue Christlikeness—the goal and prize of the Christian life. Since our goal is to be like Christ, we need to ask ourselves, *Did Christ stand firm? Did He ever waver and sin?* Scripture declares He is "without sin" (Heb. 4:15) and therefore the perfect example for us to follow.

   b) Paul's care for the church

   Paul surrounded the military command to stand firm with terms that reveal his gracious and tender spirit. His words aren't manipulative or dishonest, but a genuine expression from his heart.

12

(1) They were his love

Paul addressed the church as his "beloved brethren" (Phil. 4:1). He had a deep, holy affection for them (1:8).

It was manifested in his desire to remain with them for their "progress and joy in the faith" (1:25). Indeed, Paul was willing to be "offered upon the sacrifice and service of [their] faith" (2:17, KJV*). And only the Philippian believers had "shared with [him] in the matter of giving and receiving" (4:15), which also reveals his special bond with them.

Paul's love is also evident in the Greek term translated "whom I long to see" (*epipothētos*), which occurs only here in the New Testament and refers to the deep pain of separation from loved ones. Paul was a logician and theologian without equal—his intellectual capacity was staggering—but he was also endowed with a tremendous capacity to love people.

2) They were his joy

Certainly Paul didn't derive his joy from his circumstances—he was a Roman prisoner (1:7, 17) and the target of critics who desired "to add affliction to [his] bonds" (v. 16, KJV*).

Instead, his joy came from fellow believers. The Philippian believers were his "joy and crown" (Phil. 4:1). To the Thessalonian believers he likewise proclaimed, "Who is our hope or joy or crown of exultation? Is it not even you, in the presence of our Lord Jesus at His coming? For you are our glory and joy. . . . What thanks can we render to God

---

* King James Version.

for you in return for all the joy with which we rejoice before our God on your account?" (1 Thess. 2:19-20; 3:9). Paul rejoiced in the church's salvation, spiritual growth, and eventual perfection in Christ's presence.

(3) They were his reward

The Greek term translated "crown" refers to a laurel wreath, something an athlete received in biblical times for winning a contest (1 Cor. 9:25). But an athlete wasn't the only recipient of such a wreath. If someone was honored by his peers, he too would receive one as the guest of honor at a great feast or banquet. The wreath then was symbolic of success or a fruitful life.

It's as if Paul was saying, "The Philippian believers are my reward or trophy—proof that my efforts have been successful" (cf. 1 Cor. 9:2). That is a rich commendation.

4. The application of the command

Spiritual stability must be our objective in ministry, just as it was in the early church.

a) In Barnabas's ministry

Barnabas encouraged the church at Antioch "with resolute heart to remain true to the Lord" (Acts 11:23).

b) In Peter's ministry

Peter said, "Be on your guard lest, being carried away by the error of unprincipled men, you fall from your own steadfastness" (2 Pet. 3:17).

c) In Paul's ministry

(1) Acts 14:22—Paul was "strengthening the souls of the disciples, encouraging them to continue in the faith."

(2) Galatians 5:1—To help prevent the believers from falling back to Judaistic legalism Paul said, "It was for freedom that Christ set us free; therefore keep standing firm and do not be subject again to a yoke of slavery."

(3) 1 Thessalonians 3:8—"For now we really live, if you stand firm in the Lord." Paul received great joy from seeing stability in other believers, and so should we.

(4) 2 Thessalonians 2:15—"Stand firm and hold to the traditions which you were taught, whether by word of mouth or by letter from us." The believers weren't to waiver from the biblical truths they learned from Paul.

(5) 1 Corinthians 15:58—Paul encouraged fellow believers by saying, "Be steadfast, immovable, always abounding in the work of the Lord, knowing that your toil is not in vain in the Lord."

d) In Epaphras's ministry

Epaphras was "always laboring earnestly for [the Colossian believers] in his prayers, that [they] may stand perfect and fully assured in all the will of God" (Col. 4:12).

5. The explanation of the command

In Philippians 4:11 Paul says, "So stand firm in the Lord." The Greek term translated "so" means "thus" or "in this way," pointing to an explanation to follow. So verses 2-9, which we soon will study, tell us how to stand firm in the Lord.

1. Why do many so-called Christians refuse take a public stand for Christ (see p. 8)?
2. Why is it a battle for believers to remain stable (see pp. 8-9)?
3. In what ways was the Philippian church unstable (see p. 9)?
4. What did Christ do to keep His disciples from being unstable (see p. 9)?
5. Peter warned believers about _____ _____, who were "enticing unstable souls" (2 Pet. 2:14; see p. 9).
6. How did James describe spiritual instability (James 1:8; see p. 10)?
7. What does the life of Reuben illustrate (see p. 10)?
8. Why was the command to stand firm necessary? Support your answer with Scripture (see pp. 10-11).
9. Many believers don't take God and His commands seriously enough, wrongly regarding His commands as mere ___ ____ (see p. 12).
10. What does "therefore" in Philippians 4:1 refer to (see p. 12)?
11. How did Paul reveal his love for fellow believers (see pp. 12-13)?
12. What were Paul's circumstances when he wrote his letter (see p. 13)?
13. What was Paul's supreme joy (see p. 13)?
14. In what way were the Philippian believers Paul's "crown" (Phil. 4:1; see p. 14)?
15. Who made spiritual stability the object of ministry in the early church? Support your answer with Scripture (see pp. 14-15).
16. What does "so" in Philippians 4:1 point to (see p. 15)?

Pondering the Principles

1. The devil aggressively attacks Christians to undermine their stability. The Puritan Thomas Brooks described Satan's most devious ways of doing that: "Satan knows that if he should present sin in its own nature and dress, the soul would rather fly from it than yield to it; and therefore he presents it unto us, not in its own proper colours, but painted and gilded over with the name and show of virtue, that we may

the more easily be overcome by it, and take the more pleasure in committing of it. Pride he presents to the soul under the name and notion of neatness and cleanliness, and covetousness (which the apostle condemns for idolatry) to be but [thrift]; and drunkenness to be good fellowship, and riotousness under the name and notion of [freedom]" (*Precious Remedies Against Satan's Devices* [Edinburgh: The Banner of Truth Trust, 1987], p. 34). "Be on the alert" because "your adversary, the devil, prowls about like a roaring lion, seeking someone to devour" (1 Pet. 5:8).

2. Our pursuit of Christlikeness is the basis for standing firm in the Lord. That pursuit is eloquently depicted in the following prayer (cited from *The Valley of Vision: A Collection of Puritan Prayers and Devotions*, edited by Arthur Bennett [Edinburgh: The Banner of Truth Trust, 1989], p. 18):

> May I read the meltings of thy heart to me
> > in the manger of thy birth,
> > in the garden of thy agony,
> > in the cross of thy suffering,
> > in the tomb of thy resurrection,
> Bold in this thought I defy my adversary,
> > > tread down his temptations,
> > > resist his schemings,
> > > renounce the world,
> > > am valiant for truth.
> Deepen in me a sense of my holy relationship to thee,
> > > as spiritual bridegroom,
> > > as Jehovah's fellow,
> > > as sinners' friend.
> I think of thy glory and my vileness,
> > > thy majesty and my meanness,
> > > thy beauty and my deformity,
> > > thy purity and my filth,
> > > thy righteousness and my iniquity,
> Thou hast loved me everlastingly, unchangeably,
> > > may I love thee as I am loved;
> Thou hast given thyself for me,
> > > may I give myself to thee;
> Thou hast died for me,
> > > may I live to thee,
> > > > in every moment of my time,

17

in every movement of my mind,
in every pulse of my heart.
May I never dally with the world and its
allurements,
but walk by thy side,
listen to thy voice,
be clothed with thy graces,
and adorned with thy righteousness.

Ask the Lord to help you be like Christ.

2
Harmony and Joy

Outline

Introduction

Lesson
I. Cultivate Harmony Through Love (vv. 2-3)
    A. The Problem
    B. The Plea
    C. The People
       1. Euodia and Syntyche
       2. Suzugos
       3. Clement
       4. Other co-workers
II. Maintain a Spirit of Joy (v. 4)
    A. The Command to Rejoice
    B. The Reasons for Rejoicing

Introduction

In general our society admires those who stand true to their beliefs, who are resolute and stable under pressure. They can't be bribed, intimidated, or defeated and are looked upon as role models and leaders. Rudyard Kipling depicted such sterling character in his famous poem "If—":

If you can keep your head when all about you
    Are losing theirs and blaming it on you,
If you can trust yourself when all men doubt you,
    But make allowance for their doubting too;
If you can wait and not be tired by waiting,
    Or being lied about, don't deal in lies,
Or being hated, don't give way to hating,
    And yet don't look too good, not talk too wise:

If you can dream—and not make dreams your master;
    If you can think—and not make thoughts your aim;
If you can meet with Triumph and Disaster
    And treat those two impostors just the same.

If you can make one heap of all your winnings
    And risk it on one turn of pitch-and-toss,
And lose, and start again at your beginnings
    And never breathe a word about your loss.

If you can talk with crowds and keep your virtue,
    Or walk with Kings—nor lose the common touch,
If neither foes nor loving friends can hurt you,
    If all men count with you, but none too much;
If you can fill the unforgiving minute
    With sixty seconds' worth of distance run,
Yours is the Earth and everything that's in it,
    And—which is more—you'll be a Man, my son!

While courage, conviction, and integrity are respectable qualities from even a secular viewpoint, it is even more essential that they be manifested in the life of every Christian. That's because the name "Christian" identifies us with Christ, who never compromised or deviated from the truth. He is the perfect example of courageous integrity.

It stands to reason then that Christians are called to be stable and steadfast like Christ and not waver "like the surf of the sea driven and tossed by the wind" (James 1:6). The injunctions to stand firm (Eph. 6:11, 13-14) and be strong (1 Cor. 16:13; 2 Tim. 2:1) affirm that believers are to be bold and uncompromising in living for Jesus Christ. The apostle Paul rejoiced in seeing such stability among the Colossian believers: "Even though I am absent in body, nevertheless I am with you in spirit, rejoicing to see your good discipline and the stability of your faith in Christ" (Col. 2:5).

Most Christians earnestly desire to stand firm and not stumble in their Christian walk. No one wants to be crushed under the weight of life's trials or be defeated by the onslaught from the world, the flesh, and the devil. We all should want to hate sin the same way Paul did (Rom. 7:15). But we must realize that because we're engaged in spiritual warfare, standing firm and being strong isn't easy, (2 Tim. 2:3-4). That's why Paul uses the military term "stand firm" for the theme of spiritual stability in Philippians 4:1-9.

You might ask, "How can I be spiritually stable?" If you look at Christians around you, you'll notice some are more stable than others. That's no mystery because the Word of God openly reveals that spiritual stability is developed by adhering to certain principles. Let's look at those principles.

Lesson

I. CULTIVATE HARMONY THROUGH LOVE (vv. 2-3)

"I urge Euodia and I urge Syntyche to live in harmony in the Lord. Indeed, true comrade, I ask you also to help these women who have shared my struggle in the cause of the gospel, together with Clement also, and the rest of my fellow workers, whose names are in the book of life."

A. The Problem

Spiritual stability depends on mutual love, harmony, and peace between believers. Our lives are to be intertwined that we might support and sustain one other. Paul wanted that kind of harmony in the Philippian church, but instead there was an intense disagreement between two women threatening the church's life. Paul wanted to keep sins such as partiality, criticism, bitterness, unforgiveness, and pride from spreading throughout the church.

To avoid such problems it is necessary for believers to care and pray for each other. Mutual love produces the harmony that's conducive to spiritual stability and reflects what the church is all about: supporting the weak, lifting the fallen, and restoring the broken.

B. The Plea

In verse 2 the Greek term translated "I urge" (*parakaleō*) means "to appeal" or "entreat." It is applied to the Holy Spirit in John 14:16, whose ministry is to come alongside the believer and plead, help, or encourage. In a similar way Paul was pleading for Euodia and Syntyche "to live in harmony in the Lord."

As a great theologian and logician, Paul addressed important doctrinal issues. He opposed the legalism of the Judaizers (Phil. 3:2) and the libertine views of other false teachers (vv. 18-19). He knew such teachings perverted the doctrine of salvation and threatened the church's life. Yet he also realized that discord in the church was an equal threat to its life. That's because conflict robs the church of its power and destroys its testimony. Enemies of Christ are eager to find ways to discredit the church. Apparently the disunity in the Philippian church was about to destroy the integrity of its testimony.

Paul therefore said to them: "Conduct yourselves in a manner worthy of the gospel of Christ; so that whether I come and see you or remain absent, I may hear of you that you are standing firm in one spirit, with one mind striving together for the faith of the gospel" (1:27). "Make my joy complete by being of the same mind, maintaining the same love, united in spirit, intent on one purpose. Do nothing from selfishness or empty conceit, but with humility of mind let each of you regard one another as more important than himself; do not merely look out for your own personal interests, but also for the interests of others" (2:2-4). "Do all things without grumbling or disputing" (2:14).

C. The People

1. Euodia and Syntyche

These women were apparently leading two opposing factions in the church. We don't know what their specific complaints were, but we can surmise they weren't disagreeing over doctrine. If one were propagating error and the other the truth, the difference would have been settled quickly (cf. Gal. 1:9; Titus 3:10). So it must have been a personal conflict.

We also know the two women were prominent church members because they had worked with Paul "in the cause of the gospel" (Phil. 4:3). Normally Paul began his evangelistic efforts by visiting the local synagogue. But since the city of Philippi had no official synagogue, some faithful Jewish women met together for worship by a river. Paul "began speaking to the women who had assembled" (Acts 16:13) and shared the good news with them. That group of women might have included Euodia and Syntyche, but we really don't know.

We do know they were creating havoc in the church because it apparently was not "united in spirit [or] intent on one purpose" (Phil. 2:2). Recognizing the issue to be a lack of love—which indicates the presence of pride and the absence of humility—Paul pleaded for the women "to live in harmony in the Lord" (4:2). Each was demanding her own way rather than being concerned about the other.

"In the Lord" is the sphere where harmony is found. A right relationship with the Lord will solve any problem with discord. If two believers are walking in the Spirit, they will be right with each other.

2. Suzugos

Not only did Paul directly entreat the two women to live in harmony, but he also asked others to help them. In verse 3 the Greek term translated "comrade" (*suzug-*

os) pictures two oxen in a yoke, pulling the same load. A comrade or "yokefellow" (KJV) is a partner or equal in a specific endeavor—in this case a spiritual one. Paul added that this individual was a "true" or "genuine" comrade.

Who is this person? One possibility is an unnamed individual who was known as Paul's yokefellow. But Paul just mentioned two women by name in verse 2 and is about to name Clement in verse 3, so that seems doubtful. Another possibility is that *suzugos*—singular in number—is used in a collective sense to refer to the entire church, but that is just as doubtful.

I believe the best explanation is not to translate *suzugos* and recognize it as a proper name. So the verse would say, "Indeed Suzugos, please help these women." Who then was Suzugos? We don't know, but it's likely he was one of the church elders (1:1). So Paul was exhorting him to fulfill his duty by restoring church unity.

Paul called him a "true comrade" or Suzugos because he was living up to the meaning of his name. There are other examples in the New Testament of such men. Barnabas ("son of encouragement") genuinely encouraged believers (Acts 4:36), and Onesimus ("useful") was genuinely useful both to Paul and Philemon (Philem. 11).

Paul was asking Suzugos to be a peacemaker by helping to resolve the women's disagreement. The basis for his asking was that the women had shared Paul's struggle in advancing the gospel (Phil. 4:3). The Greek term used there (*sunathlēo*, from which we derive "athletics"), speaks of an intense struggle. That kind of effort was certainly evident at the start of the Philippian church for Paul and Silas were beaten, imprisoned, and placed in stocks (Acts 16:22-24).

3. Clement

Clement also shared Paul's struggles and probably was a church leader. He may have been the church father known as Clement I or Clement of Rome. Paul asked for his help as well in resolving the women's disagreement. We don't know anything more specific about him.

4. Other co-workers

Paul then asked for the help of "the rest of [his] fellow workers, whose names are in the book of life" (Phil. 4:3). In eternity past God registered all the names of His elect in that Book (Dan. 12:1; Mal. 3:16-17; Luke 10:20). Although their names aren't mentioned here, "God is not unjust so as to forget [their] work and the love which [they] have shown toward His name, in having ministered and in still ministering to the saints" (Heb. 6:10).

Paul wanted all the Philippian believers to experience a rich fellowship. But to achieve such harmony, each one needed to be a peacemaker by helping settle any discord.

Love is the one word summarizing every believer's duty. God loves us and we need to love one another. It's the bond that will keep the church stable.

II. MAINTAIN A SPIRIT OF JOY (v. 4)

"Rejoice in the Lord always; again I will say, rejoice!"

A. The Command to Rejoice

Many believers allow themselves to be victimized by their circumstances and consequently vacillate between a spiritual high and low. For them, a command to rejoice seems unreasonable. But the command is to rejoice "in the Lord."

We can't always rejoice in our circumstances or other people because both can be bad. However, we can rejoice in the Lord because He is always good and we know He never changes. So our spiritual stability directly relates to our knowledge of God. Knowing Him helps us live above our circumstances and provides stability. That's why the psalms were written in poetic form and meter and set to music—so the people of Israel could memorize Scripture and sing hymns to deepen their knowledge of God. Knowing Him makes everything else seem less significant.

The early church rejoiced to suffer on Christ's behalf (Acts 5:41). That kind of joy should mark us too. Romans 14:17 says, "The kingdom of God is not eating and drinking, but righteousness and peace and joy in the Holy Spirit."

B. The Reasons for Rejoicing

We should rejoice because of who God is—He is sovereign. That's the single greatest truth I know about God. Nothing is outside His control, and He controls everything to work out ultimately for our good (Rom. 8:28). He has an infinite understanding of every aspect of our lives—where we are and what we say (Ps. 139:2-4). And He exercises His understanding in perfect wisdom. Knowing God like that will give you "an inexpressible and glorious joy" (1 Pet. 1:8, NIV).

We should also rejoice because God saved us, adopted us, and promised to give us an inheritance in Jesus Christ (Eph. 1:1-11). When Christ returns, we will enjoy His presence and the heavenly place prepared for us (John 14:2-3). Until that time it's a joy to know God has promised to supply all our needs (Phil. 4:19). Furthermore, we have the privilege of serving the One we supremely love. That includes sharing the good news with the lost and encouraging fellow Christians to increase their love and service for Him. It's also a joy knowing we can pray to God at any time (Heb. 4:15-16). Finally, we can rejoice knowing that death is gain (Phil. 1:21).

The depth of our joy is directly proportional to how deeply we truly know God. And circumstances or people can't dislodge a joy that's based on who God is and what His promises are.

Focusing on the Facts

1. _____ is the perfect example of courageous integrity (see p. 20).
2. What did Paul rejoice in (Col. 2:5; see pp. 20-21)?
3. What was the problem in the Philippian church (see p. 21)?
4. What was Paul's plea in Philippians 4:2 (see p. 22)?
5. What must have been the nature of the conflict between Euodia and Syntyche? How could that be solved (see p. 23)?
6. Who is the "true comrade" in Philippians 4:3? What did Paul ask him to do (see pp. 23-24)?
7. What was the significance of sharing in Paul's "struggles" (see p. 24)?
8. Where are the names of the rest of Paul's fellow workers mentioned (Phil. 4:3; see p. 25)?
9. _____ is the one word summarizing every believer's duty (see p. 25).
10. Why do many believers vacillate between a spiritual high and low (see p. 25)?
11. Why is the command to rejoice reasonable (see p. 25)?
12. Knowing _____ helps you live above your circumstances (see pp. 25-26).
13. What are some reasons for rejoicing as a Christian (see p. 26)?

Pondering the Principles

1. The personal disagreement between two women spread discord in the Philippian church. Jonathan Edwards made this observation: "When we suffer injuries from others, the case is often such that a Christian spirit, if we did but exercise it as we ought, would dispose us to forbear taking the advantage we may have to vindicate and right ourselves. For by doing otherwise, we may be the means of bringing very great calamity on him that has injured us; and tender-

ness toward him may and ought to dispose us to a great deal of forbearance, and to suffer somewhat ourselves, rather than bring so much suffering on him. And besides, such a course would probably lead to a violation of peace and to an established hostility, whereas in this way there may be hope of gaining our neighbour, and from an enemy making him a friend" (*Charity and Its Fruits*, edited by Tryon Edwards [Edinburgh: The Banner of Truth Trust, 1986], p. 74). Make it your goal to cultivate harmony between believers through your love for them.

2. Knowing God will help you be spiritually stable. In his classic study on the topic J. I. Packer said, "Our concern must be to enlarge our acquaintance, not simply with the doctrine of God's attributes, but with the living God whose attributes they are. . . . How can we turn our knowledge about God into knowledge of God? The rule for doing this is demanding, but simple. It is that we turn each truth that we learn about God into matter for meditation before God, leading to prayer and praise to God. . . .

Meditation is the activity of calling to mind, and thinking over, and dwelling on, and applying to oneself, the various things that one knows about the works and ways and purposes and promises of God. . . . It is a matter of talking to oneself about God and oneself; it is, indeed, often a matter of arguing with oneself, reasoning oneself out of moods of doubt and unbelief into a clear apprehension of God's power and grace. Its effect is ever to humble us and to encourage and reassure us. . . . And it is as we enter more and more deeply into this experience of being humbled and exalted that our knowledge of God increases, and with it our peace, our strength, and our joy" (*Knowing God* [Downers Grove, Ill.: InterVarsity, 1973], pp. 18-19). With the Lord's help, turn your knowledge about God toward knowing God Himself.

3
Humility and Faith

Outline

Introduction
A. A Secular Perspective
B. A Biblical Perspective (Ps. 1)
    1. About stability
    2. About instability

Review
  I. Cultivate Harmony Through Love (vv. 2-3)
 II. Maintain a Spirit of Joy (v. 4)

Lesson
III. Learn to Accept Less Than You Are Due (v. 5*a*)
      A. What Forbearance Is
      B. What Forbearance Isn't
 IV. Rest on a Confident Faith in the Lord (vv. 5*b*-6*a*)
      A. The Presence of the Lord
      B. The Perplexity of Habakkuk
          1. His questions about God
          2. His knowledge of God
          3. His faith in God

Conclusion

Introduction

A. A Secular Perspective

Many people in our society want to have a more stable life. To those who are filled with anxiety and unable to cope with their circumstances, the world offers a myriad of solutions that don't work.

Unfortunately, many churches also provide the wrong solutions because they've followed after the world in believing that man can solve his deepest problems only through secular psychology. But the legacy of such philosophy and psychology is a product that can't live up to its promises. Where can you find stability to help you overcome anxiety and live above debilitating, stressful circumstances?

B. A Biblical Perspective

Let's look at Psalm 1.

1. About stability

Verses 1-3 begin, "How blessed is the man who does not walk in the counsel of the wicked, nor stand in the path of sinners, nor sit in the seat of scoffers! But his delight is in the law of the Lord, and in His law he meditates day and night. And he will be like a tree firmly planted by streams of water, which yields its fruit in its season, and its leaf does not wither; and in whatever he does, he prospers."

2. About instability

Verses 4-6 conclude, "The wicked are not so, but they are like chaff which the wind drives away. Therefore the wicked will not stand in the judgment, nor sinners in the assembly of the righteous. For the Lord knows the way of the righteous, but the way of the wicked will perish."

The person who walks with God is characterized by stability and productivity, but the one who rejects Him flounders in meaningless existence. Which would you rather be? By adhering to principles found in Philippians 4, you can learn how to be spiritually stable.

Review

I. CULTIVATE HARMONY THROUGH LOVE (vv. 2-3; see pp. 21-25)

II. MAINTAIN A SPIRIT OF JOY (v. 4; see pp. 25-26)

We can always rejoice in our privileged union with the Lord. That's illustrated by the two disciples who were walking on the road to Emmaus (Luke 24). As they were traveling, Christ met them and "explained to them the things concerning Himself in all the Scriptures" (v. 27). Later "their eyes were opened and they recognized Him; and He vanished from their sight. And they said to one another, 'Were not our hearts burning within us while He was speaking to us on the road, while He was explaining the Scriptures to us?' " (vv. 31-32). Their hearts burned because His presence was their joy.

Lesson

III. LEARN TO ACCEPT LESS THAN YOU ARE DUE (v. 5a)

"Let your forbearing spirit be known to all men."

A. What Forbearance Is

It's difficult to find one English word that captures the diverse meaning of the word translated "forbearing" (Gk., *epieikes*). Some say it speaks of contentment, gentleness, generosity, or goodwill toward others. Others say it refers to mercy or leniency toward the faults or failures of others. Still others say it speaks of patience,

31

referring to someone who submits to injustice or mistreatment, but doesn't retaliate with hatred or bitterness. I suspect the best translation is "graciousness" because in the Christian sense that word embodies all the other meanings.

But forbearance includes another important element: humility. The humble Christian says, "You mistreated, misjudged, or misrepresented me and ruined my reputation, but I trust God and don't hold a grudge against you." A person like that doesn't demand his rights. Wasn't God's grace manifested to us in the same way? After all, mankind abused and maligned Jesus Christ though He deserved none of it, yet He still reached out to man in love (cf. Rom. 5:10). Humility and graciousness will help you be stable in spite of the circumstances.

B. What Forbearance Isn't

Existentialism, the dominant philosophical mindset of contemporary psychology, has infiltrated not only our country but also many churches. It implies that every man has the right to do whatever makes him feel good. But wrong thinking like that stems from self-centered pride. It's the selfish person who says, "If something makes you feel good but hurts me, you can't do it. But if something makes me feel good but hurts you, I can do it anyway." Some deceive themselves by saying, "My sin doesn't hurt anyone," but sin always ends up hurting someone else.

Unfortunately, many Christians have become caught up in the current secular emphasis on self-esteem. Dr. Paul Brownback observed that many of today's so-called Christian books contain more about self-love than Scripture (*The Danger of Self-Love* [Chicago: Moody, 1983]). In contrast to self-love, Scripture says we're to be humble and unselfish (Phil. 2:3-4), love those who mistreat us (Matt. 5:44), and extend mercy toward those who stumble repeatedly (1 Pet. 4:8). Those qualities enabled Paul to say, "I have learned to be content in whatever circumstances I am" (Phil. 4:11). Paul was content because of his forbearing spirit, not his circumstances.

32

However, some believers take all that they hear and see and filter it through their minds to see if it wounds them in any way. But that will result in immediate instability and anxiety. When others mistreat you, humility will help you keep your balance.

IV. REST ON A CONFIDENT FAITH IN THE LORD (vv. 5b-6a)

"The Lord is near. Be anxious for nothing."

A. The Presence of the Lord

The Greek term translated "near" (*eggus*) can refer to space or time. Spatial nearness is like saying, "That chair is near." Chronological nearness is like saying, "Monday is near."

If Paul was referring to chronological nearness, this might be a reference to Christ's return. After all, Paul just said, "Our citizenship is in heaven, from which also we eagerly wait for a Savior, the Lord Jesus Christ" (Phil. 3:20). Christ's return certainly would be reason for the believers not to be anxious (4:6), but that seems a little impractical since Christ didn't return then, and the Holy Spirit, under whose inspiration Paul was writing, would have known that. Paul might have been saying the believers would see the Lord soon since life is so brief (cf. James 4:14). Both explanations could be part of what Paul was saying.

But spatial nearness seems to be the best understanding. That is, the Lord encompasses us with His presence (Ps. 119:151). When you have a thought, the Lord is near to read it; when you pray, the Lord is near to hear it; when you need His strength and power, He's near to provide it. In fact He lives in you and is the source of your spiritual life. An awareness of His presence will keep you from being anxious or unstable.

B. The Perplexity of Habakkuk

Knowing the Lord is near is meaningful only if you know the Lord. In fact, knowing God is the essence of spiritual stability because your view of God will control your conduct. The prophet Habakkuk illustrates the importance of knowing God.

1. His questions about God

Habakkuk cried out, "How long, O Lord, will I call for help, and Thou wilt not hear? I cry out to Thee, 'Violence!' Yet Thou dost not save" (Hab. 1:2). Strife and injustice had filled the land of Judah. Habakkuk wanted to know why God wasn't doing anything about it.

God responded: "Look among the nations! Observe! Be astonished! Wonder! Because I am doing something in your days—You would not believe if you were told. For behold, I am raising up the Chaldeans, that fierce and impetuous people who march throughout the earth to seize dwelling places which are not theirs.

"They are dreaded and feared. Their justice and authority originate with themselves. Their horses are swifter than leopards and keener than wolves in the evening. Their horsemen come galloping, their horsemen come from afar; they fly like an eagle swooping down to devour.

"All of them come for violence. Their horde of faces moves forward. They collect captives like sand. They mock at kings, and rulers are a laughing matter to them. They laugh at every fortress, and heap up rubble to capture it. Then they will sweep through like the wind and pass on. But they will be held guilty, they whose strength is their god" (vv. 5-11).

God was going to use a pagan nation to punish His covenant people. Habakkuk was startled: "I heard and my inward parts trembled, at the sound my lips quivered. Decay enters my bones, and in my place I tremble. Because I must wait quietly for the day of distress, for the people to arise who will invade us"

(3:16). His internal organs were shaking, his lips were trembling, and his bones were aching.

2. His knowledge of God

Habakkuk then began remembering what he knew about the Lord. He asked himself questions about God and then answered his own questions.

a) He is eternal

"Art Thou not from everlasting?" (1:12). That implies God is eternal. He is before, after, above, and independent of history, and reigning in eternal timelessness. That truth helped Habakkuk to realize everything is a part of God's majestic, eternal plan.

b) He is self-existent

"O Lord" (v. 12) is a reference to the name Yahweh, which means "I am." It tells us God is self-existent in perfect, undisturbed tranquility. He is not influenced by anything or anyone. The prophet recognized that the Lord isn't swayed by wrong information or opinions.

c) He is holy

"My Holy One" (v. 12) indicates God is perfect and must deal with sin. Indeed, Habakkuk next acknowledged, "Thine eyes are too pure to approve evil, and Thou canst not look on wickedness with favor" (v. 13). God can't act apart from His holiness that lead Habakkuk to reason this way: "I know You're punishing us because of our sin, so I know you'll punish the Chaldeans because of their sin too."

d) He is faithful

"We will not die" (v. 12) was Habakkuk's affir-
mation of God's covenant with His people. God
is faithful, true, and cannot lie.

e) He is almighty

"Thou, O Lord, hast appointed them to judge"
(v. 12) speaks of God using the Chaldeans for His
own purposes. Their devastation of Judah was
His design.

Perhaps Habakkuk was thinking, "Everything I
know about You, Lord, tells me to stop worrying
about this problem. I don't understand it, but I don't
need to. In fact, my mind is too small to do so, and
it was pride that led me to think I could."

3. His faith in God

The prophet learned a principle: "The righteous will
live by his faith" (2:4; cf. Rom. 1:17). His strong faith
in the Lord is evident in his concluding words:
"Though the fig tree should not blossom, and there
be no fruit on the vines, though the yield of the olive
should fail, and the fields produce no food, though
the flock should be cut off from the fold, and there
be no cattle in the stalls, yet I will exult in the Lord,
I will rejoice in the God of my salvation. The Lord
God is my strength, and He has made my feet like
hinds' feet, and makes me walk on my high places"
(3:17-19). In other words he was saying, "If all the
normal things of life I depend on suddenly stop, I'll
still place my hope in God. He'll give me the ability
and confidence to walk along the precipices of life's
cliffs." That is the viewpoint of a stable person.

Knowing the Lord is near helps us "be anxious for nothing" (Phil. 4:6) because we know He can handle everything.
Fretting and worrying indicate a lack of trust in God. Either
you've created another god who can't help you, or else you
believe God could help you but won't, which means you're

36

questioning His integrity and Word. So delight in the Lord and meditate on His Word (Ps. 1:2). Know who He is and how He acts. Then you'll be able to say, "The Lord is near, so I'm not going to worry."

Conclusion

Jesus said, "Do not be anxious for your life, as to what you shall eat, or what you shall drink; nor for your body, as to what you shall put on. Is not life more than food, and the body than clothing? Look at the birds of the air, that they do not sow, neither do they reap, nor gather into barns, and yet your heavenly Father feeds them. Are you not worth much more than they? And which of you by being anxious can add a single cubit to his life's span? And why are you anxious about clothing? Observe how the lilies of the field grow; they do not toil nor do they spin, yet I say to you that even Solomon in all his glory did not clothe himself like one of these.

"But if God so arrays the grass of the field, which is alive today and tomorrow is thrown into the furnace, will He not much more do so for you, O men of little faith? Do not be anxious then, saying, 'What shall we eat?' or 'What shall we drink?' or 'With what shall we clothe ourselves?' For all these things the Gentiles eagerly seek; for your heavenly Father knows that you need all these things. But seek first His kingdom and His righteousness; and all these things shall be added to you. Therefore do not be anxious for tomorrow; for tomorrow will care for itself. Each day has enough trouble of its own" (Matt. 6:25-34). What is Christ teaching us? To know and trust God, because that's the key to spiritual stability.

Focusing on the Facts

1. What words help capture the meaning of "forbearing" (Phil. 4:5)? What other important element does forbearance include (see pp. 31-32)?
2. In contrast to self-love, Scripture says we're to be _____ and _____ (see p. 32).
3. What will cause immediate instability and anxiety (see p. 33)?
4. What does the term "near" mean in Philippians 4:5 (see

pp. 33-34)?

5. _____ is the essence of spiritual stability (see p. 34).

6. Why was Habakkuk perplexed and startled? How did he deal with his feelings (see p. 34)?

7. How did knowing God is "everlasting" (Hab. 1:12) help Habakkuk (see p. 35)?

8. What is the significance of "O Lord" in Habakkuk 1:12 (see p. 35)?

9. What does "my Holy One" indicate (Hab. 1:12-13)? How would that have comforted Habakkuk (see p. 35)?

10. What principle did Habakkuk learn (Hab. 2:4)? How did he put it into practice (see pp. 36-37)?

11. Knowing the Lord helps us "be _____ _____ _____" (Phil. 4:6; see p. 37).

12. In what two ways do fretting and worrying indicate a lack of trust in God (see p. 37)?

13. What lesson is Christ teaching in Matthew 6:25-34 (see p. 37)?

Pondering the Principles

1. Forbearance (Phil. 4:5) includes the important element of humility. The Puritan Thomas Watson said this about Christ's humility: "He came not in the majesty of a king, attended with [a bodyguard], but he came poor; not like the heir of heaven, but like one of an inferior descent. The place he was born in was poor; not the royal city Jerusalem, but Bethlehem, a poor, obscure place. He was born in an inn, and a manger was his cradle, the cobwebs his curtains, the beasts his companions; he descended of poor parents. . . . He was poor, that he might make us rich. . . . He lay in the manger that we might lie in paradise. He came down from heaven, that he might bring us to heaven" (*A Body of Divinity* [Edinburgh: The Banner of Truth Trust, 1986], p. 196). Be thankful for Christ's humility on your behalf and let it motivate you to regard others as more important than yourself (Phil. 2:3), and "give preference to one another in honor" (Rom. 12:10).

2. Remembering what he knew about the Lord helped Habakkuk to strengthen his faith amidst difficult times. The Eng-

lish minister Martyn Lloyd-Jones said, "Faith, having refused to be controlled by circumstances, reminds itself of what it believes and what it knows. . . . Whatever your circumstances at this moment, bring all you know to be true of your relationship to God to bear upon it. Then you will know full well that He will never allow anything to happen to you that is harmful. 'All things work together for good to them that love God'. . . . I do not suggest that you will be able to understand everything that is happening. You may not have a full explanation of it; but you will know for certain that God is not unconcerned. That is impossible. The One who has done the greatest thing of all for you, must be concerned about you in everything, and though the clouds are thick and you cannot see His face, you know He is there" (*Spiritual Depression: Its Causes and Its Cure* [Grand Rapids: Eerdmans, 1965], p. 145). Ask the Lord to help you exercise a confident faith in Him.

4
Thankful Prayer

Outline

Introduction

Review
I. Cultivate Harmony Through Love (vv. 2-3)
II. Maintain a Spirit of Joy (v. 4)
III. Learn to Accept Less Than You Are Due (v. 5a)
IV. Rest on a Confident Faith in the Lord (vv. 5b-6a)

Lesson
V. React to Problems with Thankful Prayer (vv. 6b-7)
  A. The Attitude of the Believer (v. 6b)
  B. The Peace of God (v. 7)
    1. What it is
    2. What it does

Introduction

How can we be spiritually strong in the midst of temptations and trials? How can we be stable and not waver in the face of death? How can we be content and tranquil when grave difficulties arise? To help us be spiritually stable in such situations we need to adhere to the principles in Philippians 4:1-9.

I. CULTIVATE HARMONY THROUGH LOVE (vv. 2-3; see pp. 21-25)

II. MAINTAIN A SPIRIT OF JOY (v. 4; see pp. 25-26)

III. LEARN TO ACCEPT LESS THAN YOU ARE DUE (v. 5*a*; see pp. 31-33)

The humble believer realizes his unworthiness to have received God's grace. And since God's grace is sufficient for every situation in life, He's not expecting or making demands for anything better. Such an outlook will help any believer be stable, even when despised or rejected by others.

IV. REST ON A CONFIDENT FAITH IN THE LORD (vv. 5*b*-6*a*; see pp. 33-37)

David wrote, "In Thee, O Lord, I have taken refuge; let me never be ashamed; in Thy righteousness deliver me. Incline Thine ear to me, rescue me quickly; be Thou to me a rock of strength, a stronghold to save me. For Thou art my rock and my fortress; for Thy name's sake Thou wilt lead me and guide me. Thou wilt pull me out of the net which they have secretly laid for me; for Thou art my strength. Into Thy hand I commit my spirit; Thou hast ransomed me, O Lord, God of truth" (Ps. 31:1-5). His trust rested in the character of God. An adequate knowledge of God is essential for spiritual stability. And the only way to know God is through what He has chosen to reveal of Himself in Scripture.

Just as the Lord was David's confidence in physical battle, so He is our confidence in spiritual battle. Ephesians 6:15 says we're to "shod [our] feet with the preparation of the gospel of peace" for spiritual warfare against the devil and his forces. Roman soldiers wore hobnail boots made of leather. The nails were driven through from the inside, enabling the soldier to anchor his boot in the soil to prevent slipping or sliding during life-and-death combat. In the same way the gospel of peace helps us stand firm in spiritual warfare. Knowing God is on our side is the anchor of our confidence in battle, for He is our friend, resource, and power.

A Comparison of Two Theologies

Through the years Arminian and Calvinistic theologies have been at opposite poles. Traditional reformed theology that we call Calvinism emphasizes God's sovereignty, but Arminian theology in effect emphasizes man's sovereignty. That is the primary difference. Arminian theology teaches that God is helpful in providing spiritual assistance, but that one must find it in himself to come to Christ, persevere in the faith, accomplish spiritual goals, and win spiritual victories.

What results from that kind of theology? First, a person can profess to trust in Christ, but in reality trust in himself. That's illustrated by someone who says, "I had the sense to commit my life to Christ." Those words reflect the belief that the power to choose salvation—or lose it through spiritual failure—belongs to the individual. But can you imagine facing death, believing you had that kind of power, and wondering what your standing with God was? Can you imagine the battle in your heart over the issue of your salvation, not knowing if you committed too many sins to be disqualified from heaven? That kind of uncertainty will bring anxiety, not security.

An understanding of God's sovereignty will help a believer be stable. And fully trusting God requires an understanding of His sovereign grace: that an individual is chosen, redeemed, kept, and glorified *by God*, who is the initiator. That means every trial of the believer's life is under God's sovereign control to perfect him or her for His eternal purpose and glory.

Another result of man-centered theology is the belief that Christians can bind Satan and demons. But that kind of power hasn't been given to believers. Even the archangel Michael, "when he disputed with the devil and argued about the body of Moses, did not dare pronounce against him a railing judgment, but said, 'The Lord rebuke you' " (Jude 9). God alone is the One who controls Satan. Those who practice such things have an exalted view of themselves, not understanding their own weakness or the greatness of God's power.

Lesson

V. REACT TO PROBLEMS WITH THANKFUL PRAYER (vv. 6b-7)

A. The Attitude of the Believer (v. 6b)

"In everything by prayer and supplication with thanksgiving let your requests be made known to God."

We've already talked about the virtues of peace, love, joy, humility, and faith. Here we see the virtue of gratitude—the antidote to worry—is to be our attitude in prayer. The Greek terms used refer to specific petitions made to God in the midst of difficult times.

Instead of praying to God with doubt or discontentment, the believer is to approach God in a spirit of thanksgiving. That's because God promised not to allow anything into our lives that will be too much for us to bear (1 Cor. 10:13), to work out everything for our good in the end (Rom. 8:28), and to "perfect, confirm, strengthen and establish" us in the midst of our suffering (1 Pet. 5:10).

The believer is to know that all difficulties are within God's purpose and to thank Him for His available power and promises. First Peter 5:7 says, "Cast all your anxiety on him because he cares for you" (NIV). In doing so we are to be thankful for His providence, His promise of perfecting us, the glory He will receive from accomplishing His will, and for past mercies that are the promise of future blessings.

Being thankful releases us from fear and worry. The presence of worry could mean a believer doesn't understand who God is, or else has a weak faith because of sin in his life. We need to trust every situation to God's sovereign control. If we understand that God will supply all our needs (Phil. 4:19), and that He knows everything about our lives (Ps. 139:3), cares about us (1 Pet. 5:7), has the power to overcome for every difficulty

44

(Ps. 62:11), is perfecting us to be like Christ (Phil. 1:6), and that nothing escapes Him (Ps. 147:5), that will lead us to be stable, not anxious.

B. The Peace of God (v. 7)

"The peace of God, which surpasses all comprehension, shall guard your hearts and your minds in Christ Jesus."

1. What it is

This verse promises inner calm or tranquility to the believer who prays with a thankful attitude. Notice it doesn't promise what the answer to our prayers will be.

The apostle Paul has been building a spiritual crescendo: as you cultivate love and peace in the fellowship (vv. 2-3), focus on your relationship to the living Christ (v. 4), have a humble heart and derive comfort from the nearness of God (v. 5), and pray with a thankful heart in the midst of difficulties (v. 6), God will respond by giving you His peace (cf. Isa. 26:3). This peace "surpasses all comprehension," which speaks of its divine origin. It transcends human intellect, analysis, and insight. No human counselor can give it to you because it's a gift from God.

The real challenge of Christian living is not to eliminate every uncomfortable circumstance from your life but to trust the infinite, holy, sovereign, and powerful God in the midst of every situation. So the way you look, the way you've been treated by others, or where you live or work isn't the issue.

Jesus said, "These things I have spoken to you, that in Me you may have peace. In the world you have tribulation, but take courage; I have overcome the world" (John 16:33). So we need to live on the supernatural plane, accept that we live in a fallen world, and allow God to do His perfect work in us. And God will give us His peace as we confidently entrust ourselves to His care.

2. What it does

The peace of God "shall guard your hearts and your minds in Christ Jesus" (Phil. 4:7). The Greek term translated "shall guard" is a military term meaning "to keep watch over." The Philippian believers lived in a garrison town where Roman soldiers were stationed to guard the interests of the empire in that part of the world. In the same way, God's peace guards us from anxiety, doubt, fear, and distress.

John Bunyan's *The Holy War* illustrates how the peace of God watches over the believer's heart. In the allegory, Mr. God's-Peace was appointed to guard the city of Mansoul. As long as Mr. God's-Peace ruled, Mansoul enjoyed harmony, happiness, joy, and health. However, Prince Emmanuel (Christ) went away because Mansoul grieved him. Consequently, Mr. God's-Peace resigned his commission and chaos resulted.

The believer who doesn't live in the confidence of God's sovereignty will lack God's peace and be left to the chaos of a troubled heart. But our confident trust in the Lord will allow us to thank Him in the midst of trials because we have God's peace on duty to protect our hearts.

The apostle Paul isn't making a distinction between the heart and mind. Although we could say the heart is the seat of personhood and the mind is the seat of thought, I think he's making a comprehensive statement that refers to the whole inner person. Because of our union with Christ, He guards our entire inner being with His peace. And that's what helps us be spiritually stable.

Focusing on the Facts

1. What will help you be stable when rejected or despised by others (see p. 42)?

2. How did David manifest his confident faith in God (Ps. 31:1-5; see p. 42)?
3. What is the only way we can know God (see p. 42)?
4. What does it mean to "shod your feet with the preparation of the gospel of peace" (Eph. 6:15; see pp. 42-43)?
5. What must the believer understand to fully trust God (see p. 43)?
6. What specific virtue is to characterize the believer's prayers (Phil. 4:7; see p. 44)?
7. What divine promises help remove doubt and discontentment from the believer's life (see p. 44)?
8. What are two specific reasons for the presence of worry (see p. 44)?
9. What does verse 7 promise those who pray with thankfulness? What doesn't the verse promise (see p. 45)?
10. What does "surpasses all comprehension" mean (v. 7; see p. 45)?
11. What is the real challenge of Christian living (see p. 45)?
12. What does "shall guard" mean in verse 7? What is the believer guarded from (see p. 46)?
13. The believer who doesn't live in the confidence of God's ____ ____ will lack God's peace (see p. 46).
14. What is the significance of our union with Christ (see p. 46)?

Pondering the Principles

1. God promises to guard our hearts and minds with peace as we entrust ourselves to His care (Phil. 4:7). God's peace was especially evident in the life of Madam Guyon. After spending ten years in a dungeon far below the surface of the ground lit only by a candle at meal times, she wrote these words (cited by A. W. Pink in *The Sovereignty of God* [Grand Rapids: Baker, 1930], p. 191):

A little bird I am,
Shut from the fields of air;
Yet in my cage I sit and sing
To Him who placed me there;
Well pleased a prisoner to be,
Because, my God, it pleases Thee.

Nought have I else to do
I sing the whole day long;
And He whom most I love to please,
Doth listen to my song;
He caught and bound my wandering wing
But still He bends to hear me sing.

My cage confines me round;
Abroad I cannot fly;
But though my wing is closely bound,
My heart's at liberty.
My prison walls cannot control
The flight, the freedom of the soul.

Ah! it is good to soar
These bolts and bars above,
To Him whose purpose I adore,
Whose Providence I love;
And in Thy mighty will to find
The joy, the freedom of the mind.

Ask the Lord to help you trust His sovereign care for every situation.

2. The believer is to pray with an attitude of "thanksgiving" (Phil. 4:6). The Dutch minister Frans Bakker wrote, "True thankfulness begins by recognizing our weakness. It ends in praising God, glorifying His Name, and praising His attributes in love. A mark of true thankfulness is that we love the giver more than the gifts. When God's creatures return to Him, there in His presence His goodness is experienced. If we possess this love we always have something to be thankful for" (*Praying Always*, translated by Cornelis and Fredrika Pronk [Edinburgh: The Banner of Truth Trust, 1987], p. 85). Read 1 Chronicles 16:8-36 and "ascribe to the Lord the glory due His name" (v. 29).

5
Godly Thinking

Outline

Introduction

Review
I.   Cultivate Harmony Through Love (vv. 2-3)
II.   Maintain a Spirit of Joy (v. 4)
III. Learn to Accept Less Than You Are Due (v. 5a)
IV.   Rest on a Confident Faith in the Lord (vv. 5b-6a)
V.   React to Problems with Thankful Prayer (vv. 6b-7)

Lesson
VI.   Focus on Godly Virtues (v. 8)
    A. How We Think
        1. Before salvation
        2. At salvation
        3. After salvation
            a) Our minds have been transformed
            b) Our minds need regular cleansing
    B. What We Should Think About
        1. Truthful things
        2. Noble things
        3. Righteous things
        4. Pure things
        5. Gracious things
        6. Praiseworthy things

Conclusion

Introduction

God is calling us to be spiritually stable, firm, and strong. But how can we be triumphant instead of defeated? How can we be joyous and not depressed? By adhering to the principles in Philippians 4:1-9.

Review

I.   CULTIVATE HARMONY THROUGH LOVE (vv. 2-3; see pp. 21-25)

II. MAINTAIN A SPIRIT OF JOY (v. 4; see pp. 25-26)

III. LEARN TO ACCEPT LESS THAN YOU ARE DUE (v. 5a; see pp. 31-33)

IV. REST ON A CONFIDENT FAITH IN THE LORD (vv. 5b-6a; see pp. 33-37)

V.   REACT TO PROBLEMS WITH THANKFUL PRAYER (vv. 6b-7; see pp. 44-46)

We should be thankful knowing God uses every situation to accomplish His purposes. Romans 8:28 says He "causes all things to work together for good to those who love God, to those who are called according to His purpose." We should also be thankful for conforming us to be like His Son and His care for us. And we have His promise of future deliverance into His eternal presence. So we have many reasons for being thankful.

The prophet Jonah reacted with thankful prayer when he was swallowed by the great fish (Jonah 2:1). Now if you suddenly found yourself in a fish's belly, how would you react? Maybe you'd cry out, "What are You doing, God? Where are You? Why is this happening?" But Jonah reacted differently: "I called out of my distress to the Lord, and He answered me. I cried for help from the depth of Sheol; Thou didst hear my voice. For Thou hadst cast me into the deep, into the heart of the seas, and the current engulfed me. All Thy breakers and billows passed over me" (vv. 2-3). He told of his sinking into the sea.

Then Jonah said, "I have been expelled from Thy sight. Nevertheless I will look again toward Thy holy temple. Water encompassed me to the point of death. The great deep engulfed me, weeds were wrapped around my head. I descended to the roots of the mountains. The earth with its bars was around me forever" (vv. 4-6). Perhaps he thought God might not know where he was.

Nevertheless in the midst of such great trauma Jonah prayed with thanksgiving: "Thou hast brought up my life from the pit, O Lord my God. While I was fainting away, I remembered the Lord; and my prayer came to Thee, into Thy holy temple. Those who regard vain idols forsake their faithfulness, but I will sacrifice to Thee with the voice of thanksgiving. That which I have vowed I will pay. Salvation is from the Lord" (vv. 6-9). Although he had his weaknesses, Jonah reflected great spiritual stability in his prayer. He was confident of God's ability to deliver him if He so chose. In the same way the peace of God will help us be stable if we react to circumstances with thankful prayer.

Lesson

VI.   FOCUS ON GODLY VIRTUES (v. 8)

"Whatever is true, whatever is honorable, whatever is right, whatever is pure, whatever is lovely, whatever is of good repute, if there is any excellence and if anything worthy of praise, let your mind dwell on these things."

This verse is the climax of how to be spiritually stable. That's because spiritual stability is the result of how we think. Focusing on godly virtues produces love, joy, humility, faith, and gratitude (vv. 2-7). The Greek term translated "let your mind dwell on" (*logizomai*) speaks of mental reflection that affects one's conduct.

51

We are the products of our thinking. Proverbs 23:7 says, "As [a person] thinks within himself, so he is." Unfortunately, many modern psychologists believe an individual can find stability by recalling his past sins, hurts, and abuses. That kind of thinking has also infiltrated Christianity. However, Philippians 4:8 says we're to focus only on what is right and honorable, not on the sins of darkness (cf. Eph. 5:12).

Pursue Right Thinking

It's frightening to realize our culture has more interest in emotion and pragmatism than in thinking. That's evident when people more often ask, "How will it make me feel?" instead of "Is it true?" That wrong focus is also evident in today's theology, where the predominant questions are "Will it divide?" and "Will it offend?" rather than "Is it right?" The people of Berea were "noble-minded" because "they received the word with great eagerness, examining the Scriptures daily" (Acts 17:11). They were interested in finding truth, not good feelings or pleasant circumstances.

In his book *Right Thinking* Bill Hull says, "What scares me is the anti-intellectual, anti-critical-thinking philosophy that has spilled over into the church. This philosophy tends to romanticize the faith, making the local church into an experience center. . . . Their concept of 'church' is that they are spiritual consumers and that the church's job is to meet their felt needs" ([Colorado Springs: Navpress, 1985], p. 66). Many people are going to church not to think or reason about the truth, but to get a certain feeling.

But living by emotions rather than right thinking will produce instability. In his book *Your Mind Matters* John Stott says, "Sin has more dangerous effects on our faculty of feeling than on our faculty of thinking, because our opinions are more easily checked and regulated by revealed truth than our experiences" ([Downers Grove, Ill.: InterVarsity, 1973], p. 16). So it's important for the Christian not to fall victim to his feelings.

The Critical Issue Is How You Think

Traditional psychiatry sees man at the pinnacle of an evolutionary process, yet having many of the same characteristics as less-advanced species. That's why many believe the results of Pavlov's famous stimulus-response experiment with dogs are true for humans as well. However, psychiatrist William Glasser, the father of reality therapy, comes up with a different conclusion in his book *Stations of the Mind* ([New York: Harper and Row, 1981]).

In his study of how the brain works, he discovered that man isn't controlled by a predictable stimulus-response factor, but by internal wants and desires. According to Glasser what man wants is predetermined by what influences him—that is, his thinking. His study shows man's response to outside stimuli is not mechanical, but thoughtful because the mind is the command center determining conduct. Glasser concluded that the critical issue is how man thinks since that is what influences his actions.

From the biblical perspective the importance of how we think is very clear. In Isaiah 1:18 the Lord says, "Come now, and let us reason together." In Matthew 16:1-4 Christ tells the religious leaders not to look for a sign, but to think about the facts already revealed in Scripture (cf. Luke 12:54-57; 16:29-31). And here in Philippians 4:8 Paul issues a call for godly thinking.

A. How We Think

1. Before salvation

   a) Romans 1:28—"As they did not see fit to acknowledge God any longer, God gave them over to a depraved mind." Our minds were corrupt.

   b) 2 Corinthians 4:4—"The god of this world has blinded the minds of the unbelieving." Our minds were blind.

   c) Ephesians 4:17—"Walk no longer just as the [lost] also walk, in the futility of their mind." Our minds were engaged in futile thoughts.

   d) Ephesians 4:18—The ungodly are "darkened in their understanding, excluded from the life of God, because of the ignorance that is in them." Our minds were ignorant.

e) 1 Corinthians 2:14—"A [lost] man does not accept the things of the Spirit of God; for they are foolishness to him, and he cannot understand them, because they are spiritually appraised." Our minds were foolish.

Since the mind of the lost is corrupt it doesn't choose what is good, since it is blind it doesn't know what is good, since it is futile it doesn't perform what is good, and since it is ignorant it doesn't even know it's doing any of that. The thinking of fallen man is foolish indeed.

2. At salvation

a) 1 Peter 3:15—"Always be prepared to give an answer to everyone who asks you to give the reason for the hope that you have" (NIV). The believer should be able to explain his faith to the lost because the Lord uses the gospel to illuminate the mind of the unbeliever.

b) Matthew 13:19—"When anyone hears the word of the kingdom, and does not understand it, the evil one comes and snatches away what has been sown in his heart." The lost must understand God's Word to receive salvation. That's why Romans 10:17 says faith comes by hearing—understanding—about Christ. Salvation begins in the mind as an individual understands the truth about his sin and Christ's atoning work on his or her behalf.

c) Luke 10:27—"You shall love the Lord your God with all your heart, and with all your soul, and with all your strength, and with all your mind." Salvation involves an intelligent response and a reasonable trust in the revealed truth about God.

d) Matthew 6:26—Jesus said, "Look at the birds of the air, that they do not sow, neither do they reap, nor gather into barns, and yet your heavenly Father feeds them. Are you not worth much more than they?"

In his book *The Sermon on the Mount* Martyn Lloyd-Jones says, "Faith, according to our Lord's teaching in [Matthew 6:25-34], is primarily thinking. . . . We must spend more time in studying our Lord's lessons in observation and deduction. The Bible is full of logic, and we must never think of faith as something purely mystical. We do not just sit down in an armchair and expect marvelous things to happen to us. That is not Christian faith. Christian faith is essentially thinking. Look at the birds, think about them, and draw your deductions. Look at the grass, look at the lilies of the field, consider them. . . .

"Faith, if you like, can be defined like this: It is a man insisting upon thinking when everything seems determined to bludgeon and knock him down in an intellectual sense. The trouble with the person of little faith is that, instead of controlling his own thought, his thought is being controlled by something else, and, as we put it, he goes round and round in circles. That is the essence of worry. . . . That is not thought; that is the absence of thought, a failure to think" (vol. 2 [Grand Rapids: Eerdmans, 1960], pp. 129-30). Faith isn't psychological self-hypnosis or wishful thinking, but a reasoned response to revealed truth.

Some people assume worry is the result of too much thinking. But in reality it's the result of too little thinking in the right direction. If you know who God is and understand His purposes, promises, and plans, it will help you not to worry.

3. After salvation

    a) Our minds have been transformed

    In regeneration we receive a new mind or way of thinking. Our human thought patterns are injected with divine and supernatural ones.

    1) Romans 8:5-6—"Those who are according to the flesh set their minds on the things of the

55

flesh, but those who are according to the Spirit, the things of the Spirit. For the mind set on the flesh is death, but the mind set on the Spirit is life and peace." Because of the Spirit of God in our lives, we think on a spiritual level, not a fleshly one.

2) 1 Corinthians 1:30—"By His doing you are in Christ Jesus, who became to us wisdom from God, and righteousness and sanctification, and redemption." Since God imparts His wisdom to us, we can think the deep thoughts of the eternal God (cf. Ps. 92:5).

3) 1 Corinthians 2:11-12—"The thoughts of God no one knows except the Spirit of God. Now we have received, not the spirit of the world, but the Spirit who is from God, that we might know the things freely given to us by God." Because the Holy Spirit indwells us, we have the very thoughts of God available to us.

4) 1 Corinthians 2:15-16—"He who is spiritual appraises all things, yet he himself is appraised by no man. For who has known the mind of the Lord, that he should instruct Him? But we have the mind of Christ." The Spirit gives us understanding about God.

5) 1 Corinthians 10:15—The apostle Paul said, "I speak as to wise men; you judge what I say." Paul had to deal with some major problems in the Corinthian church, such as their desecration of the Lord's Table (11:20-22). But by God's grace the Corinthian believers had received divine wisdom to evaluate and understand their situation. Their thinking was to be consistent with God's wisdom, which they received in Christ.

b) Our minds need regular cleansing

Because we live in a fallen world our renewed minds need ongoing cleansing and refreshment. God's chief agent of purifying our thinking is His Word (John 15:3; Eph. 5:26).

1) Colossians 3:10—"Put on the new self who is being renewed to a true knowledge according to the image of the One who created him."

2) Romans 12:1-2—Paul said, "I urge you therefore, brethren, by the mercies of God, to present your bodies a living and holy sacrifice, acceptable to God, which is your spiritual service of worship. And do not be conformed to this world, but be transformed by the renewing of your mind, that you may prove what the will of God is, that which is good and acceptable and perfect."

3) Ephesians 4:23—"Be renewed in the spirit of your mind."

4) 1 Thessalonians 5:21—"Examine everything carefully; hold fast to that which is good."

The New Testament calls us to the mental discipline of right thinking. Colossians 3:2 says, "Set your mind on the things above, not on the things that are on earth." First Peter 1:13 says, "Gird your minds for action, keep sober in spirit, fix your hope completely on the grace to be brought to you at the revelation of Jesus Christ."

And Paul often said in his letters, "I would not . . . that ye be ignorant" (Rom. 11:25; 1 Cor. 10:1; 2 Cor. 1:8; 1 Thess. 4:13, KJV) and "know ye not" (Rom. 6:3, 16; 1 Cor. 3:16; 2 Cor. 13:5, KJV). He was concerned that believers think rightly. When Christ spoke He used the term translated "think" to help His listeners have the right focus (Matt. 5:17; 18:12; 21:28; 22:42).

The Old Testament also calls us to right thinking. King Solomon said, "My son, if you will receive my sayings, and treasure my commandments within you, make your ear attentive to wisdom, incline your heart to understanding; for if you cry for discernment, lift your voice for understanding; if you seek her as silver, and search for her as for hidden treasures; then you will discern the fear of the Lord, and discover the knowledge of God. For the Lord gives wisdom; from His mouth come knowledge and understanding" (Prov. 2:1-6).

Dwelling on the right things takes initiative and effort—just as it does when mining for silver. But if we're faithful to make the maximum effort, God will give us understanding (cf. Ps. 119:34).

B. What We Should Think About

Philippians 4:8 says to dwell on "whatever is true . . . honorable . . . right . . . pure . . . lovely . . . of good repute . . . [excellent, and] worthy of praise."

1. Truthful things

We will find what is true in God's Word. Jesus said, "Sanctify them in the truth; Thy word is truth" (John 17:17; cf. Ps. 119:151). The truth is also in Christ: "You did not learn Christ in this way, if indeed you have heard Him and have been taught in Him, just as truth is in Jesus" (Eph. 4:20-21). And the truth is also in God: "With gentleness [correct] those who are in opposition, if perhaps God may grant them repentance leading to the knowledge of the truth" (2 Tim. 2:25). Dwelling on what is true necessitates meditating on God's Word.

2. Noble things

The Greek term translated "honorable" means "worthy of respect" and refers to that which is noble, dignified, and reverent. We are to think about whatever is worthy of awe and adoration—the sacred as opposed to the profane.

3. Righteous things

The term "right" speaks of righteousness. Our focus is to be in perfect harmony with the eternal, unchanging, divine standard of the holy God revealed in Scripture. Right thinking is always consistent with God's absolute holiness.

4. Pure things

The term "pure" refers to something morally clean and undefiled. We are to dwell on what is clean, not soiled.

5. Gracious things

The Greek term translated "lovely" (*prosphilēs*) occurs only here in the New Testament and means "pleasing" or "amiable." The implication is we are to focus on whatever is kind or gracious.

6. Praiseworthy things

The Greek term translated "good repute" speaks of that which is highly regarded or well thought of. Whereas "honorable" predominantly refers to something worthy of veneration by believers, this term refers to what is reputable in the world at large, such as kindness, courtesy, and respect for others.

Focusing on godly virtues will affect what you decide to see (such as television programs, books, or magazines) and say (perhaps to friends or those at work). That's because your thinking affects your desires and behavior. It's as if Paul was saying, "Since there are things out there that are excellent and worthy of praise, please focus on them."

Conclusion

In verse 9 Paul concludes, "The things you have learned and received and heard and seen in me, practice these things; and the God of peace shall be with you." He was saying, "I'm an example of one who focuses on godly virtues. If you follow my example, you'll have not only the peace of God (v. 7) but also the God of peace" (v. 9). Paul maintained spiritual stability in the midst of severe trials (vv. 11-13), and you can too by following his example.

Focusing on the Facts

1. Describe how Jonah responded to his severe trial (Jonah 2:1-9; see pp. 50-51).
2. Why is Philippians 4:8 the climax of how to be spiritually stable (see p. 51)?
3. Why were the people of Berea "noble-minded" (Acts 17:11; see p. 52)?
4. How did you think before salvation? Support your answer with Scripture (see pp. 53-54).
5. What does the Lord use to illuminate the mind of an unbeliever (1 Pet. 3:15; see p. 54)?
6. Salvation begins in the mind as an individual understands the truth about his _____ and Christ's _____ _____ (see p. 54).
7. What is faith according to Matthew 6 (see p. 55)?
8. In salvation you receive a new mind. Support that truth with Scripture (see pp. 55-56).
9. What does the Lord use to cleanse and refresh the believer's mind (see p. 57)?
10. What does Proverbs 2:1-6 teach (see p. 58)?
11. Where can you find truth? Support your answer with Scripture (see p. 58).
12. What does "right" refer to in Philippians 4:8 (see p. 58)?
13. Why will focusing on godly virtues affect what you see and say (see p. 590)?
14. What is Paul an example of in verse 9 (see p. 60)?

1. The Puritan John Owen used an analogy to show the importance of continually—not just occasionally—focusing on spiritual things: "The thoughts of spiritual things are with many, as guests that come into an inn, and not like children that dwell in the house. They enter occasionally, and then there is a great stir about them, to provide [suitable] entertainment for them. In a while they are disposed of, and so depart, being neither looked nor inquired after any more. Things of another nature are attended to; new occasions bring in new guests, for a season. [However, children that dwell in the house] are missed if they are out of the way, and have their daily provision constantly made for them. So it is with these occasional thoughts about spiritual things. By one means or other they enter into the mind, and there are entertained for a season. On a sudden they depart, and men hear of them no more. But those that are natural and genuine, arising from a living spring of grace in the heart, disposing the mind unto them, are as the children of the house; they are expected in their places, and at their seasons. If they are missing, they are inquired after. The heart calls itself to an account, whence it is that it hath been so long without them, and calls them over [for a desired conversation] with them" (*The Grace and Duty of Being Spiritually Minded* [Grand Rapids: Baker, 1977], pp. 62-63). Make this your prayer: "Let the words of my mouth and the meditation of my heart be acceptable in Thy sight, O Lord, my rock and my Redeemer" (Ps. 19:14).

2. In his book *Spiritual Intimacy* Richard Mayhue wrote, "To hear something once for most of us is not enough. To briefly ponder something profound for most of us does not allow enough time to grasp and fully understand its significance. This proves to be most true with God's mind in Scripture. The idea of meditating sometimes lends itself to misunderstanding, so let me illustrate its meaning. . . . For me, the most vivid picture comes from a coffee percolator. The water goes up a small tube and drains down through the coffee grounds. After enough cycles, the flavor of the coffee beans has been transferred to the water which we then call coffee. So it is that we need to cycle our thoughts

through the 'grounds' of God's Word until we start to think like God" ([Wheaton, Ill.: Victor, 1990], pp. 46-47). Renew your mind by regularly meditating on God's Word. Doing so will bring into your mind what is spiritually healthy and lead you away from what is harmful.

6
Obedience

Outline

Introduction
A. The Stresses of Life
   1. David's experience
   2. A depressed pastor's experience
B. The Testimony of the Believer

Review
I.   Cultivate Harmony Through Love (vv. 2-3)
II.   Maintain a Spirit of Joy (v. 4)
III. Learn to Accept Less Than You Are Due (v. 5a)
IV.   Rest on a Confident Faith in the Lord (vv. 5b-6a)
V.   React to Problems with Thankful Prayer (vv. 6b-7)
VI.   Focus on Godly Virtues (v. 8)

Lesson
VII. Obey God's Standard (v. 9)
A. The Practice of the Believer
   1. What "practice" means
   2. What the believer is to practice
      a) Things learned
      b) Things received
      c) Things heard
      d) Things seen
B. The Peace of God

Conclusion

Introduction

A. The Stresses of Life

1. David's experience

Out of his deep distress David prayed, "O Lord, rebuke me not in Thy wrath; and chasten me not in Thy burning anger. For Thine arrows have sunk deep into me, and Thy hand has pressed down on me. There is no soundness in my flesh because of Thine indignation; there is no health in my bones because of my sin. For my iniquities are gone over my head; as a heavy burden they weigh too much for me. My wounds grow foul and fester. Because of my folly, I am bent over and greatly bowed down; I go mourning all day long. For my loins are filled with burning; and there is no soundness in my flesh.

"I am benumbed and badly crushed; I groan because of the agitation of my heart. Lord, all my desire is before Thee; and my sighing is not hidden from Thee. My heart throbs, my strength fails me; and the light of my eyes, even that has gone from me. My loved ones and my friends stand aloof from my plague; and my kinsmen stand afar off. Those who seek my life lay snares for me; and those who seek to injure me have threatened destruction, and they devise treachery all day long" (Ps. 38:1-12).

Because of his sin, David was experiencing the heavy weight of guilt and divine chastisement. His friends offered no help or encouragement, and his enemies wanted to kill him. Feeling utterly forsaken, he trusted the Lord to answer his prayer and not forsake him (vv. 15, 21).

2. A depressed pastor's experience

Such affliction was not unique to David. A pastor wrote this account of turmoil in his own life: "I had visited Ward 7E many times. Its institutional yellow walls and highly polished floors resembled most of the psychiatric wards and mental hospitals where I had gone to minister to members of my congregation.

"There's always a certain apprehension that lurks in the shadow of one's mind while walking down those sterile, silent corridors. Behind each door is a different story. I've listened to them all. The criminally insane, the suicidal, the depressed, the alcoholic, the hostile, the addict, and then on many occasions I've tried to talk to those who have forgotten how to respond.

"I've never felt comfortable with the mentally ill. This time, however, my discomfort had been replaced by fear. My apprehension had given way to feelings of impending doom. The very atmosphere was charged with foreboding glimpses of the unpredictable. I was traumatized with humiliation and embarrassment. I was struggling against a creeping hostility waiting to overpower me. This time I was being led down the silent halls of Ward 7E, not as a pastor but as a patient.

"For years I had struggled to understand the unpredictable mood swings that could carry me from peaks of elation to the deep valleys of despair. I could preach with fervor and power, I could share Christ with enthusiasm and success. I would counsel with meaningful insight and socialize with sheer delight.

"But without warning, any or all of these positive and delightful emotions would suddenly be forced to give way to feelings of gloom and periods of weakness. I would withdraw, and a form of paranoia would settle in. I would suddenly be overwhelmed with feelings of inadequacy and inferiority. On occasion I toyed with thoughts of self-destruction" (Don Baker and Emery Nester, *Depression* [Portland: Multnomah, 1983], pp. 15-16).

B. The Testimony of the Believer

Were the experiences of David and the pastor isolated instances? Maybe there have been times when you also felt crushed, weak, and unable to stand. Perhaps you know what it's like to lose your spiritual balance. We face strong temptations and trials in this life. Nevertheless, it's important for us to be spiritually stable not only for our own well-being but also for our Christian testimony before the lost world.

Unbelievers find it difficult to understand how the Christian who believes in an all-sufficient God can live as though God were not just that. Martyn Lloyd-Jones said, "Now we believe that God extends His Kingdom partly through His people, and we know that He has oftentimes done some of the most notable things in the history of the Church through the simple Christian living of some quite ordinary people. Nothing is more important, therefore, than that we should be delivered from a condition which gives other people, looking at us, the impression that to be a Christian means to be unhappy, to be sad, to be morbid, and that the Christian is one who 'scorns delights and lives laborious days' " (*Spiritual Depression: Its Causes and Its Cure* [Grand Rapids: Eerdmans, 1990], p. 11).

The believer who is spiritually stable has a testimony that honors Christ. That's the kind of testimony the apostle Paul had. Bound in chains as a prisoner of the Roman Empire, he remained content and confident in the Lord (Phil. 4:11, 13). You can have that same stability by heeding the principles in verses 1-9.

Review

I. CULTIVATE HARMONY THROUGH LOVE (vv. 2-3; see pp. 21-25)

II. MAINTAIN A SPIRIT OF JOY (v. 4; see pp. 25-26)

III. LEARN TO ACCEPT LESS THAN YOU ARE DUE (v. 5a; see pp. 31-33)

IV. REST ON A CONFIDENT FAITH IN THE LORD (vv. 5b-6a; see pp. 33-37)

V.   REACT TO PROBLEMS WITH THANKFUL PRAYER (vv. 6b-7; see pp. 44-46)

VI. FOCUS ON GODLY VIRTUES (v. 8; see pp. 51-60)

Lesson

VII. OBEY GOD'S STANDARD (v. 9)

"The things you have learned and received and heard and seen in me, practice these things; and the God of peace shall be with you."

A. The Practice of the Believer

1. What "practice" means

The Greek term translated "practice" (*prassō*) speaks of action that's repetitious or continuous. For example, we say that someone practices the violin or tennis. That's using the word in the sense of working on a skill to improve it. When we say a doctor or lawyer has a practice, we are referring to his normal routine of life. Similarly, the word here refers to one's pattern of life or conduct.

The godly conduct that produces spiritual stability depends on obeying the divine standard of God's Word. The Word is what cultivates godly attitudes, thoughts, and actions that will keep you from being overwhelmed by trials and temptations.

Arresting the Flesh

To understand the relationship between godly attitudes, thoughts, and actions, consider this analogy. If a policeman sees someone who's about to violate the law, he will arrest that person. Similarly, godly attitudes and thoughts produced by the Word act as policemen to arrest the flesh before it commits a crime against the standard of God's Word. But if they aren't on duty, they can't arrest the flesh, and the flesh is free to violate the law of God.

67

The analogy teaches that right attitudes and thoughts must precede right practices. Paul understood only spiritual weapons will help in our warfare against the flesh (2 Cor. 10:4). By using the right weapons, we can take "every thought captive to the obedience of Christ" (v. 5).

Pure behavior produces spiritual peace and stability, but sinful behavior produces instability. Isaiah 32:17 says it like this: "The work of righteousness will be peace, and the service of righteousness, quietness and confidence forever." That is true not only in the millennial kingdom, where Christ one day will rule the earth in righteousness, but also in the life of the believer. James said, "The wisdom from above is first pure, then peaceable. . . . And the seed whose fruit is righteousness is sown in peace by those who make peace" (James 3:17-18).

Contentment, comfort, calm, quietness, and tranquility accompany godly conduct, which is based on God's Word. Doing good is not only the way to overcome evil (Rom. 12:21) but also the expected practice of every believer. As godly habits are cultivated by the power of God, bad habits will diminish and the believer's life becomes more and more stable.

2. What the believer is to practice

In Philippians 4:9 Paul says, "The things you have learned and received and heard and seen in me, practice these things." The Philippian believers had the Old Testament books to go to, but the entire New Testament hadn't been completed at the time Paul wrote this letter. Since they may have had access to only a minimal amount of written revelation in the New Testament, the believers looked to the apostles as their source of truth until all the New Testament books were brought together. So the standard of Christian belief and behavior was embodied in the teaching and example of the apostles.

That's why on the day of Pentecost three thousand believers "were continually devoting themselves to the apostles' teaching" (Acts 2:42). That's also why Paul said to the Corinthian believers, "Be imitators of me, just as I also am of Christ" (1 Cor. 11:1) and why he told the

Philippian believers to practice what they had learned, received, heard, and seen in his life (Phil. 4:9).

a) Things learned

The Greek term translated "learned" (*mathanō*) is a derivative of "disciple" and speaks of teaching and instructing. Paul was referring to what they learned from his personal instruction, which included preaching, teaching, and discipling (cf. Acts 20:20). He expounded Old Testament truths and the meaning of New Testament revelation, explaining how it applied to their lives.

That personal instruction was especially evident as Paul and Timothy ministered together. Timothy patterned his life after Paul's "teaching, conduct, purpose, faith, patience, love, [and] perseverance" (2 Tim. 3:10). Paul was a living illustration that the apostles were not only to reveal the truth but also to live it (cf. Phil. 3:17).

b) Things received

This speaks of direct revelation from God. Scripture makes it clear that Paul received direct revelation from the Lord and then made it known to the believers.

1) 1 Corinthians 11:2—"Hold firmly to the traditions, just as I delivered them to you."

2) 1 Corinthians 15:1-3—"I make known to you, brethren, the gospel which I preached to you, which also you received, in which also you stand. . . . For I delivered to you as of first importance what I also received."

3) Galatians 1:9—"As we have said before, so I say again now, if any man is preaching to you a gospel contrary to that which you received, let him be accursed."

4) 1 Thessalonians 4:1—"We request and exhort you in the Lord Jesus, that, as you received from us instruction as to how you ought to walk and please God (just as you actually do walk), that you may excel still more."

5) 1 Timothy 6:20—"Guard what has been entrusted to you."

6) 2 Timothy 2:2—"The things which you have heard from me in the presence of many witnesses, these entrust to faithful men, who will be able to teach others also." Those who received God's Word from Paul were to deliver that same Word to the next generation. And the revealed Word has continued from one generation of faithful believers to the next.

c) Things heard

This refers to what the Philippian believers heard about Paul from sources other than Paul himself (his personal instruction to them) or God (His direct revelation, which passed from Paul to the believers). Certainly the Philippian believers had heard about his character, lifestyle, and preaching from others and were aware of his impeccable reputation. So Paul wasn't afraid in telling them to practice what they had heard about his life.

d) Things seen

This refers to what the Philippian believers knew to be true about Paul from firsthand experience. Paul knew the apostles were to walk with Christ and be living models of New Testament Christianity before the early church.

Certainly Paul exemplified the spiritual fruit of peace, joy, humility, faith, and gratitude. And he dwelled on what was true, honorable, right, pure, lovely, and of good repute. So he wasn't embarrassed to tell the believers to practice what they had seen in his life.

Today we have the completed New Testament as the divine pattern for our conduct. But that doesn't mean those who preach, teach, and represent the New Testament are permitted to live any way they want. Even though we're not apostles, our lives are to be worthy of imitation by other believers. We're to be like the man who built his house on the rock (Matt. 7:24). That is, we need not only to hear the Word but also to act on what we've heard. "Prove yourselves doers of the word, and not merely hearers who delude themselves" (James 1:22).

B. The Peace of God

Philippians 4:9 concludes, "The God of peace shall be with you." "The God of peace" speaks of the God whose character is peace. He is the origin and giver of peace. Paul ended on this note because he was addressing the issue of spiritual stability in the midst of trials. When we have godly attitudes, thoughts, and actions, the peace of God and the God of peace will guard us. His peace provides comfort, tranquility, quietness, and confidence.

Paul often referred to the Lord as the God of peace. In Romans he said, "Now the God of peace be with you all. . . . The God of peace will soon crush Satan under your feet" (15:33; 16:20). In 2 Corinthians he wrote, "The God of love and peace shall be with you" (13:11). And to the Thessalonian believers he said, "May the God of peace Himself sanctify you entirely. . . . Now may the Lord of peace Himself continually grant you peace in every circumstance" (1 Thess. 5:23; 2 Thess. 3:16).

Conclusion

Godly attitudes, thoughts, and actions require spiritual discipline. Martyn Lloyd-Jones said, "I defy you to read the life of any saint

71

that has ever adorned the life of the Church without seeing at once that the greatest characteristic in the life of that saint was discipline and order. Invariably it is the universal characteristic of all the outstanding men and women of God. Read about Henry Martyn, David Brainerd, Jonathan Edwards, the brothers Wesley, and Whitfield—read their journals. It does not matter what branch of the Church they belonged to, they have all disciplined their lives and have insisted upon the need for this; and obviously it is something that is thoroughly scriptural and absolutely essential" (*Spiritual Depression*, p. 210). Through spiritual discipline you will find strength and contentment for every situation in life.

Focusing on the Facts

1. When he felt utterly forsaken, David _____ the Lord (see p. 64).
2. Why is it important to be spiritually stable (see p. 66)?
3. What does "practice" in Philippians 4:9 mean (see p. 67)?
4. What does godly conduct depend on (see p. 67)?
5. How can believers keep the flesh from violating the law of God (see pp. 67-68)?
6. Believers are to take "every thought captive to the _____ of Christ" (2 Cor. 10:5; see p. 68).
7. _____ produces spiritual peace and stability (see p. 68).
8. Why did the believers look upon the apostles as models of Christian belief and behavior (see p. 68)?
9. How was direct revelation made known to the Philippian believers (see pp. 69-70)?
10. What did the Philippian believers hear about Paul (see p. 70)?
11. What is the divine pattern for Christian conduct today (see p. 71)?
12. How can your life be worthy of imitation by other believers (see p. 71)?
13. Where must we go to find peace (see p. 71)?
14. Godly attitudes, thoughts, and actions require _____ (see p. 72).

Pondering the Principles

1. King Josiah became ruler of Judah at the age of eight. Read 2
    Kings 22:1–23:25 and answer the following questions.

    - What was Josiah's spiritual condition (22:2)?

    - Why was Judah the object of God's wrath (22:13, 17)?

    - What was Josiah's attitude toward God's Word (22:19)?

    - When King Josiah heard God's Word, how did he react
      (23:2-3)?

    - In what way did King Josiah manifest obedience to
      God's Word (23:5-15)?

    - How does Scripture assess King Josiah's life (23:25)?

    Let the life of Josiah encourage you to obey God's Word.

2. Philippians 4:9 connects godly living with God's peace.
    Read Proverbs 1:33 and 28:1 to see that connection as well.
    Then write Philippians 4:6-9 on a card and memorize it.
    Ask for the Lord's help in overcoming worry and meditate
    upon the memorized Scripture when tempted. Doing so
    will reinforce godly thinking and living.

Scripture Index

Topical Index